# SCHIRMER'S LIBRARY
OF MUSICAL CLASSICS

SELECTED SONATINAS

For the Piano

IN THREE BOOKS

→ **Book I: ELEMENTARY**
Library Vol. 1594

Book II: INTERMEDIATE
Library Vol. 1595

Book III: LOWER ADVANCED
Library Vol. 1596

ISBN 978-0-7935-5194-1

G. SCHIRMER, Inc.

DISTRIBUTED BY

HAL•LEONARD®
CORPORATION
7777 W. BLUEMOUND RD. P.O. BOX 13819 MILWAUKEE, WI 53213

LIST OF COMPOSERS

Beethoven, Ludwig van (1770-1827)

Clementi, Muzio (1752-1832)

Dussek, Johan Ladislaus (1760-1812)

Gurlitt, Cornelius (1820-1901)

Haydn, Joseph (1732-1809)

Kuhlau, Friedrich (1786-1832)

Lichner, Heinrich (1829-1898)

Mozart, Wolfgang Amadeus (1756-1791)

Reinecke, Carl (1824-1910)

Spindler, Fritz (1817-1905)

HINTS ON HOW TO STUDY A SONATINA

1. Determine the key of each movement.

2. Number each measure of each movement.

3. Determine the length of the phrases.

4. Subdivide the phrases (where they can be subdivided).

5. Note that often the answering phrase corresponds to the first phrase in rhythmic and melodic pattern, with a change of cadence. (The term cadence-chord refers to the final chord of a phrase.)

6. First Movement: Study the two subjects of the Exposition. Label the key of the second subject and mark the connecting links. The purpose of the link or Transition is to lead away from the first subject and the home key. If there is a full close or half close at the end of the first subject, it is an easy matter to determine where the Transition begins. The modern composers do not use the formal cadence but lead directly into the other subjects. The second subject usually consists of two or more ideas and is longer than the first subject. Before you can determine the second subject, you may have to find it in the home key in the Recapitulation.

7. (First Movement:) Is Part 2 a Development Group or an Episode? In a Development Group the tonic key is avoided by frequent and unexpected modulations. An easily recognized rhythmic figure taken from the Exposition is often used.

8. (First Movement:) Mark the closing of Part 2 and the preparation for the return of the first subject.

9. (First Movement:) To find the Coda, look for the point at which the recapitulation of the subjects ceases. It seldom contains new material.

10. The slow movement has no set form, but is often ABA with Coda or Theme and Variations.

11. For the last movement, the old or the new Rondo form is often used, or the First-Movement form. A few composers have used Theme and Variations.

12. Indicate how you would lay out an orchestral arrangement of one of the sonatinas.

A SONATA QUIZ

1. What does the word "sonatina" mean?
   Ans.: "Little sonata", or a sonata that is relatively short, easy, or light.

2. Can a hard and fast line be drawn between "sonatas" and "sonatinas"?
   Ans.: No. It is largely a matter of what the composer wants to call his work.

3. What does "sonata" mean?
   Ans.: A piece that is "sounded" or played instrumentally, rather than being *cantata* or "sung"

4. Bach called many of his instrumental pieces "suites". How does a suite differ from a sonata?
   Ans.: Suites are usually in the same key throughout, and most of the movements are named according to certain dances. Sonatas are usually *not* in the same key throughout, and usually have a tempo-indication rather than the name of a dance at the beginning of each movement.

5. Who is credited with having finally established the piano sonata as a definite form?
   Ans.: Clementi.

6. Clementi once engaged in a musical contest with Mozart in Vienna. Who won the contest?
   Ans.: Neither; the winner was left undecided. But Clementi later said that from that time on he adopted a new style of playing—which indicates that he perhaps considered Mozart the victor.

7. What did Mozart think of Clementi?
   Ans.: Mozart said that Clementi was "strong in runs of thirds, but without a pennyworth of feeling or taste".

8. Who was the first composer to distinguish the style of the pianoforte from that of the harpsichord in his compositions?
   Ans.: Clementi.

9. Besides being a pianist and composer for the piano, Kuhlau played and composed for what other instrument?
   Ans.: The flute.

10. When Kuhlau once made a visit to Beethoven, what musical game did they play?
    Ans.: They made up humorous canons. One of Beethoven's, beginning *Kuhl, nicht lau* ("Cool, not lukewarm") is still preserved.

11. The Viennese Classical period in music began about 1760. Who were three great composers of this school?
    Ans.: Haydn, Mozart, and Beethoven.

12. What was Haydn's contribution to the sonata form?
    Ans.: Regularity and sharpness in the building of subjects.

13. What are the main qualities of Mozart's sonatas?
    Ans.: Fluency, clearness, and beauty of melody.

14. How does Beethoven's treatment of the sonata differ from his predecessors'?
    Ans.: He is more concerned with content than with form.

15. The 48 Preludes and Fugues of Bach have been compared to the Old Testament; what then would be the New Testament?
    Ans.: The 32 piano sonatas of Beethoven.

CONTENTS

SONATINA.

CARL REINECKE. Op. 136, № 1.

SONATINA.

CARL REINECKE. Op.136, No 2.

Allegro moderato.

Piano

Menuetto.

Rondino.
Vivace.

SONATINA.

FRITZ SPINDLER. Op. 157, N⁰ 4.

Moderato.

Piano

Vivo.

Sonatina

H. Lichner. Op. 49, Nº 1

39898

SONATINA.

C. GURLITT. Op. 54, No 4.

Allegro non troppo.

Piano

f risoluto.

Adagio molto sostenuto.

con gran espressione.

con gran espress.

Allegretto scherzando.

SONATINA.

Op. 88, № 1.

Fingered and phrased by
LUDWIG KLEE.

FR. KUHLAU.

Allegro (♩ = 126)

SONATINA.

Op. 38, No 3.

MUZIO CLEMENTI

Allegro (♩ = 126)

Allegretto (♩. = 72)